Discover

by

ISBN 978-1-932336-44-3

Published by Spiritual Dynamics Academy LLC

First published: January 6, 2008
Updated: June 14, 2022

Infinite ∞ ***Being***

Clear and Concise Metaphysical Insights

Table of Contents

Introduction

Just imagine what it will be like to wake up every morning and know that you hold the key to the very reason for life itself. Not just to your own purpose, but the master key to the very reason for the existence of the universe!

When you gain this profound depth of understanding, imagine the sense of purpose and destiny that will be yours each and every day!

Discovering your personal purpose in life will be relatively easy, once you understand the basics. This book, however, doesn't stop there. It will take you far beyond basic knowledge and into a place that, until recently, no one has ever reached!

You are about to discover the answer to the deepest secret in the universe. The reason why the universe was created in the first place.

You are about to discover the reason *why* life exists.

When you become aware of the deepest reason for life itself, then everything else falls into place. Suddenly, everything about your life makes perfect sense. Your own purpose in life takes on a clarity and a meaning that was never before so apparent.

Purpose And Destiny

What is your purpose in life?

You can probably sense that you have a purpose, in which case you know intuitively that one exists. The challenge is, bringing that information forward into your conscious awareness so that you can confidently act upon it each and every day.

Your purpose in life is real... very real. And, unique.

The knowledge of your purpose in life exists at a deeper level of awareness than your daily consciousness, so that is exactly where you go to find it.

In this book, we'll see how you can take that exact journey. We will also be going *deeper into why* you have a purpose in life. And, thanks to the efforts of a certain angelic helper, deeper than any book in recorded history has ever done!

Purpose and destiny are closely related. The purpose of your life is the theme that runs throughout your life. Your destiny is the plan that you, at a soul level, made for yourself to act upon that theme.

We will see how destiny began with your own pre-life planning; with a collection of intended experiences that you carefully previewed, at a soul level of consciousness, before you were born into this life.

You may have had one or more déjà vu experiences in your life. These are experiences where you feel or see something for the first time and, yet, it feels as if you have already had the experience. For example, you may walk into a new house for the first time and yet you feel as if you have been to this house and seen it before.

It is as if your memory has been jogged, but how could it be a memory? Did you dream this before you actually experienced it? How does this happen, and, more importantly, *why* does it happen? We'll explore this concept later in the book, as we unravel the mechanism behind the phenomenon of déjà vu.

As you know, your conscious mind is just one part of your full range of consciousness. It is focused upon the external world and upon the information that you are constantly fed through your physical senses. The conscious part of your mind is designed for a very specific task. It enables you to focus upon, and act out, experiences upon the theater-like stage that we call life.

The conscious mind, with its precise awareness of the concepts of space and time, makes physical life appear solid and real; even though, as we all know, matter is made of energy, and, is therefore not really as solid as it would appear to be.

It is the job of your subconscious mind to expertly manage the functions of your physical body. It also contains the full memory of every experience you, as a soul, have ever had since time began.

While your subconscious mind remembers everything about the past, it is the superconscious part of your mind which looks forward in time. It is here, in the superconscious, that you are fully aware of the fine details of your personal destiny.

Your superconscious mind is also known as your soul, higher self, or inner self. The term *inner self* illustrates the nature of the superconscious mind compared to the conscious mind which, with its focus upon the external world, acts as an *outer self*.

At the level of consciousness of your inner self, you have some very definite plans as to what you want to experience and achieve in this life. The moment you turn your attention within through meditation, or simply by letting your outer self go to sleep at night, your awareness is free to expand to encompass more of your inner self. It is in these deeper states of consciousness that you are aware that, at a soul level, you have made some very definite plans for your life.

However, your self-made life plan faces an ongoing challenge. You, at your soul level of consciousness, before you incarnated, made the best possible plan for the life ahead. You chose your parents based on who they are, where they lived, and how they would affect your life as a growing child. You set up strategic links with other souls so that you would meet people who were key to your plan as your life progresses. All of this intense planning occurred before you breathed your first breath as a new-born infant and transferred your focus into the physical world. So, the original plan was made before you were born, for what was seen as the probable future that existed at that time.

The problem is, the future is a fickle thing. It can change like the wind, and often does. Future events can materialize in ways different from the likely outcomes that you pre-viewed at the time.

How do you prevent the calamity of your best-laid plans becoming derailed? We'll get to that a little later, but first, let's go deeper into the whys and wherefores of destiny and purpose.

Looking Deeper For The Reason Why

If destiny and purpose both exist, why? Is there a reason behind their existence?

Both destiny and purpose are mapped out at a soul level, but what lies beyond the soul? What motivates the soul? Why did you, at a soul level of consciousness, feel impelled to plan anything at all? Why not just cruise through life and see what happens? Is there some deep yearning behind the need for a purpose in life and a plan of action to act out that purpose?

What lies beyond the soul level of consciousness? Is it a straight run from there to the ultimate state of God-consciousness, or is there some stairway to heaven in existence, with each step on the stair being one stage further along the way?

We'll be looking into the structure of the various layers of consciousness that exist, but first, let's examine the mathematical, statistical proof that there really is God at the end of the stairs.

After all, in order to solve the riddles of deeper consciousness, there is one prerequisite. A belief in the existence of a Creator. A belief that the universe as we know it was carefully designed, placed into perfect balance, and intended into existence.

As long as you think there is a reason behind life, then, *w*hen you ask the question, "Why?", you can go one level deeper into the reasons behind the mysteries of life.

We'll be asking *why* several times, each time triggering an exploration into a deeper level of existence.

When the universe came into existence, it unfolded into a perfect working order. For this to happen, it required a perfectly balanced set of conditions to unfold into perfect order rather than random chaos.

In his book, *The Life of the Cosmos*, physicist Lee Smolin details the many variables which had to be exactly balanced in order for the universe to unfold into such living order. The mass of the proton, the strength of gravity, the range of the weak nuclear force, and dozens of other variables determine how an emerging universe will unfold.

If any of these values at all had been just slightly different, the universe would have become a disorganized pool of hot plasma where galaxies and solar systems were unable to form.

In order to make a universe that supports life, the numbers have to be exactly right. What are the mathematical chances of a universe forming that is in perfect order and capable of supporting life as we know it?

One chance in 10^{229}.

That's one chance in 10 to the power 229.

Or, to spell it out, that's exactly one chance in...

10,000,000,000,000,000,000,000,000,000,000,0
00,000,000,000,000,000,000,000,000,000,000,0
00,000,000,000,000,000,000,000,000,000,000,0
00,000,000,000,000,000,000,000,000,000,000,0
00,000,000,000,000,000,000,000,000,000,000,0
00,000,000,000,000,000,000,000,000,000,000,0
00,000,000,000,000,000,000,000,000,000.

Basically, then... no chance at all!

Therefore, God must exist.

Today's Challenges

Your destiny in this life will be closely woven into your cultural environment. Not just the influences of your family, friends and teachers, but also the challenges that society faces.

The Shift is the spiritual and creative awakening of humanity. This ongoing transformation has gained momentum in recent years to the point where, today, more than one in four adults have moved forward towards this new stage of cultural awareness.

The Shift is a movement from a society filled with hierarchy and control to one motivated by heart-centered consciousness. Society is about to morph into one which promotes unconditional love, personal empowerment, and a work ethic of service to others rather than self-centered gain.

Ironically, adopting an ethic of service to others produces more, not less, prosperity for an individual, but the person has to first shift to heart-centered consciousness to see this unfold in practice. First, they have to really want to help others; then the magic happens.

Today, society exists in a pressure cooker of rapid change. Every year that goes by seems to go by faster. We are under enormous pressures from all directions, to the point where it is often hard to just stop and think for a minute before going on with the next hectic task on an endless list of activities.

Later in the book, we will see how this pressure towards chaos will likely play out and what it will mean to spiritual seekers and to your purpose in life.

First, though, let's find out more about the people we love.

In Pursuit Of Happiness

Why are some people that you know more special than anyone else in the world?

We need to take a moment to go beyond external appearances and recall the inner connection that we share with the people around us. Recalling that inner connection is not hard. At night, in the deepest level of sleep, you reconnect with your soul family and thrill at the union that you all share.

Soul families consist of people who resonate to the same 'musical tone' of consciousness as each other. Each person has a *signature tone* of consciousness which represents uniquely who they are. People of like mind and consciousness resonate easily together.

When you move up through the spirit realms at night to meet people in your soul family, you know them by the unique signature tone of consciousness that radiates from them. It doesn't matter how their spiritual body appears to your sense of spiritual vision, you know them by how their unique consciousness signal, their signature tone, feels to you.

Each person belongs to a primary group of soul mates which, typically, numbers around eight souls. This primary group vibrates in close harmony with other groups which, in turn, vibrate in close harmony with still more groups. The number of people in your extended soul family can easily stretch to two thousand or more individuals.

Among these, especially the closer ones, are the people that you interact with in meaningful ways as you pass through life on Earth together. Actually, when you plan your life as a soul before you begin your life, part of that planning is to arrange to meet like-minded friends who will help you through significant events and experiences in that life.

Part of your consciousness lives with the pure essence of your soul family all the time, not just at night when the main focus of your attention rises through the spirit realms to meet them. It is your awareness of that soul family-connected part of yourself which makes you yearn for the close community that you experience in that realm of consciousness.

Friends and family members who have always seemed especially close seem that way because you share a common resonance. This is a typical sign of soul family relationships.

Both small soul groups and large soul families have their own themes that they are exploring. Today, The Shift is the big event that attracts most of the attention in life-planning sessions, but how you personally choose to explore The Shift is highly variable.

Your immediate soul group may have one theme that it wants to focus upon, while your larger soul family has another theme running in the background. Because of the harmony that exists between the groups that make up the soul family, there will be harmony in the different themes. They will intertwine with each other, simply because, to a large extent, you all have like-minded interests.

There are many people in the world who are truly close to you at a soul family level. The fact that people have a fundamental need for love, acceptance and friendship makes this very reassuring as we pass through the cross-currents of daily living.

For the truly curious, let's stop now for a moment and ask why we have a fundamental need for love and acceptance, just to see where it leads.

This is a need for love and unity. It might seem unusual to ask why we have such a need, but, when you do, this question leads to deeper truths about your purpose in life.

The Universal Yearning For Unity

Within us all lies a Universal Yearning for Unity consciousness, a yearning to return to that from which we came. This all-pervasive yearning for unity constantly calls us towards our spiritual home. As a sentient being in a world of separate beings, your primary mission has always been to find your way back to your spiritual source, to that original state of consciousness where All is One.

Despite the distractions of physical life, despite its noise and clatter, you have a silent, inner drive which keeps your soul wanting to travel back towards its original source. Deep within, you have a yearning to be reconnected with the unity from which you once came.

This Universal Yearning for Unity, the UYU (*"you-you"*), leads us ever onwards, towards our eventual, spiritual homecoming and into complete unity. You have an eventual destiny where all things come back together into one whole, but, getting back to the present, what about your identity as an individual today?

What about your unique personality, the carefully crafted character that has evolved in this lifetime? There has to be a reason for the infinite diversity of humankind, or such a thing wouldn't exist.

Infinite Diversity

If, deep down, we want to become one with others, then why is everyone unique? Why is everyone different from everyone else?

Your primary purpose in life is to experience life from one individual, unique point of view. Just as each snowflake is unique, so is each person. That's the way life was designed. You are an expression of Infinite Being as it experiences itself from all possible viewpoints.

Infinite Being created infinite diversity in order that an infinite variety of experience may be gained. This is why there are as many paths to spiritual oneness as there are humans upon the face of the Earth.

Modern day humanity will reach unity and a lasting world peace when, paradoxically, people accept the diversity of humanity. There will never be a one-size-fits-all, world religion which demands the conformity of everyone, simply because one size of anything never did fit all people. What there will be is a worldwide acceptance of human diversity and the fact that there is a limitless variety of spiritual paths back to Infinite Being, the one source of all life.

The freedom to pursue your own unique path back to original oneness is a fundamental right endowed upon you by the Creator of all life. As a living being, you have the inalienable right to be who you are, and definitely not what someone else wants you to be.

As we move away from the Old Reality and further into New Reality consciousness, it is appropriate to celebrate our uniqueness and the individual paths that we have chosen to tread. Life is a cycle of experience and its ultimate purpose is to learn how to reconnect with the spiritual joy which radiates from within our inner beings.

As humans, we need to honor the uniqueness of ourselves and, indeed, everyone. Shortly, we will discuss how to discover and develop the full potential within your unique personality.

Along the way, we will also see why there is a drive within humanity for greater understanding, and see why that is an essential part of the growth of humanity.

First, however, let's answer one fundamental question. If, ultimately, the mind of God is all that exists, then how was the physical universe created from just consciousness and nothing else?

The Conscious Universe

The term *Infinite Being* as the ultimate state of consciousness is one which is representative of a greater concept of God. Some people call this greater concept *The Absolute*, or *The All That Is*. The term *Infinite Being* is one that precisely describes the original consciousness which underlies all of Creation.

The universe was created within the consciousness of Infinite Being. The universe is held within that immense, all-encompassing oneness. Now, as consciousness is the only tool available to the Original Creator, the universe must be made of 100% consciousness. So, solid matter, including your desk, your phone and your chair, are really made up of consciousness which is held in tension in order to have the appearance of solidity.

When the Original Creator aspect of Infinite Being came forth into existence, it did so by moving consciousness into motion. It began, initially, by projecting pure thought in one direction. By *thought*, I mean intellect - the kind of thought-process that an architect uses to create a building. Only, in this case, a universe was about to appear.

The second facet of Original Consciousness was pure feeling. As we will see later, this was projected sideways, at a ninety-degree, right-angle to pure thought. Finally, motion brought a complex dance of thought and feeling into play, and, then, all else became possible.

In the human realm, we do not experience the extremes of pure thought and pure feeling like the Original Creator does. Our thoughts and feelings are always intertwined. Like the electric and magnetic energies in electromagnetism, which is light energy, one always invokes the other. In humans, a thought causes feelings to arise. A feeling causes thoughts to arise.

In the realm of Original Creation, however, pure thought and pure feeling do exist as complementary principles, just like the pure electric and pure magnetic components exist within electromagnetic, or light, energy.

Thought plus feeling in motion is the underlying formula in the creation of a conscious universe.

But, for the truly curious, that raises an even deeper question; and one which is, in this case, the ultimate question in life.

Why did Infinite Being want to create the universe in the first place?

Why did life begin? Not *how* did life begin, but *why?*

In the beginning, before the universe was created, there was only pure consciousness. This was the ultimate, original consciousness of God, existing in perfect, blissful beingness. Then, this Infinite Being, this All That Is, decided to create life so that living beings could search for the perfection that once was; so that living beings could find their way back home to their perfect source.

But, why would Infinite Being begin a journey to search for what it already has? Why would Infinite Being involve itself into matter, then work its way back to itself in pursuit of perfection, bliss and completion, when it already was all of that?

For thousands of years, mystics have searched for the answer to this deepest of all mysteries. Now, finally, one of them has found the answer. But, in order to find it, first he had to die!

The Ultimate Question

Why did life begin?

What *preceded* the creation of the physical universe? Long before all the details were thought about, Infinite Being made the initial move from pure beingness into the very earliest form of initial action.

Why, when Infinite Being was perfection, bliss, and completion in every way, did it want to move from just *being* into an active state of *doing*?

I remember, in the 1970's, a lecture by George King (1919-1997), a renowned Master of Kundalini Yoga. He said that this was the ultimate question on Earth, and it was a question to which no one on Earth had the answer. Here was a man who had studied Eastern esoterica since his early years, fully mastered Kundalini Yoga, and spent countless hours in the ultimate state that anyone can reach while living in a physical body: Cosmic consciousness.

I remember my feeling of disappointment when I heard him say that no one had the answer to that question. Here was a teacher from whom I had learned deeper truths than from any other source to date and, if he said that no one on Earth had the answer, then it seemed to me that the ultimate question would remain a mystery.

Ancient Hindu texts talk of God breathing out into Creation, and then breathing back in on the return journey to itself, gaining perfection as it did. But no one knew why God had decided to venture forth from pure beingness and into action.

As I was writing this book in December 2007, I was sadly reflecting on the fact that the answer to the ultimate question was not to be found anywhere and, at the same time, remembering those words from my favorite teacher, back in the days when I was a lot younger, but just as curious. George King had passed away ten years before, so I couldn't exactly lift the phone and say, "Do you have an update on that?"

Why would Infinite Being embark upon a journey in search of perfection when it already had perfection? This is the question that has stymied mystic philosophers throughout the history of humankind on Earth. This is the question that has made thinkers shake their heads in frustration at the impasse which blocks their way.

This is the mystery which has, up until now, prevented us from knowing the answer to the question;

"Why we are here?"

It hasn't ever been my habit to look for answers from spirit guides. Rather, it has always been my style to search my own inner space looking for inspiration. If someone from the afterlife were to come down from the spirit realms to visit me in my study, I'd be quite surprised at such an unexpected visit.

On that day, I was lost in my reflections about the ultimate question when, suddenly, that's exactly what happened! A spirit presence materialized right in front of my desk. I double-blinked my eyes, but to no avail, because physical eyes don't see spirit bodies. However, the sense of his presence was unmistakable, as was his identity.

Here was a presence of the oversoul of the late George King. In response to my reflections, my curiosity, and my contemplative thoughts about him, he had come to visit.

I was halfway through recovering from the surprise when the thought, "I've cracked the code" came into my head, as clear as day.

"What?" I responded, then immediately knew what he meant, as if an understanding had just unfolded into my consciousness.

"I found the answer", he clarified and, again, a set of related information unfolded itself into my awareness.

Shortly after his passing on from the physical realm ten years before, he had established residency among colleagues in what he calls Level

Six of the Earth. The physical realm is Level Three, or the third density layer of the twelve layers that exist. To put that in perspective, Infinite Being is beyond the twelfth, i.e. beyond all the layers of its own Creation.

So, George King now has a three-level advantage when it comes to the starting realm for his meditative research. From Level Six, he had gone into a state of meditation that went far beyond anything attainable in this physical world. And, he'd found the answer to why God had created the universe in the first place!

"What is it?", I gasped in surprise, and promptly received an assurance that it was something quite simple. Actually, when you think about it, an ultimate reality has to be ultimately simple.

"What was the answer?", I thought, almost bursting with intense curiosity.

Right there, very appropriately, he dropped the answer into my thought stream.

"Curiosity was the first seed of action."

Infinite Being, in its ultimate peace, bliss and completeness in all ways, had initially developed a spark of curiosity! That was the one, initial catalyst through which all else had come into being.

Curiosity had led to the desire to explore, for Infinite Being to begin to see itself from different viewpoints and to see where that would lead.

The great journey from being to doing had begun in that embryonic seed of curiosity.

The outbreath into Creation had begun and it would continue, driven by the power of curiosity, until the inbreath would eventually bring all of Creation back to its spiritual roots, enriched by having gained an infinite variety of experiences.

Curiosity was the earliest motivator in the history of Creation. Life began with curiosity.

Two minutes before, I'd been wondering what the answer could possibly be. Now I wondered why I had ever wondered! It seemed so obvious, once I'd been shown the answer.

Curiosity – the one attribute that drives progress; that drives learning. Curiosity – the one quality we possess that shows we are well and truly a creation of our Creator.

We were made in the image of God; in the imagination of the Creator. We were provided with intelligence, love, self-direction, and – the engine that powers us along the journey back to our Spiritual Home – curiosity.

This is what drives humanity on a perpetual quest for greater understanding of all aspects of life.

Curiosity is the relentless drive that is a built into us all. It is curiosity that is an essential part of the growth of humanity.

So, thanks to *George King* – the man who truly has gone where no one has gone before – you and I now have the 'key to the castle,' the answer to the most fundamental question in the universe.

Now, we are able to work forward from that most fundamental of all places and see how the answers to all of those other questions fall into place. First, however, we need to be aware of The Great Paradox of Infinite Being.

The Great Paradox Of Infinite Being

Infinite Being is The One and The All. We are aspects of the One, aspects of Infinite Being, each of us experiencing life from our own unique perspective. This concept leads to the idea that you are one small part of an infinitely large variety of life. However, when you go within and contact the deeper levels of consciousness, you begin to sense that that concept is actually one of the illusions of life as we know it.

Infinite Being is The One and The All. We can see the Infinite variety of The All in the external world but, at the deepest level of consciousness, each individual part of The All is The One.

At the deepest level, you are not a ***part*** of The One. Within the One, there are no parts. There is no separation. Within the One, you ***are*** The One. You are Infinite Being.

If this were not so, then at that deepest level of awareness, there would be both The One and you. That would make two, and that is not what is there at that deepest level of consciousness. Only The One exists in that ultimate state. Therefore you are The One, as, indeed, is everyone else.

Infinite Being is The One and The All.

We are Infinite Being.

So, The Great Paradox of Infinite Being is this: While you appear to be one of infinite parts of The All, at the deepest level of awareness you are not a separate part. You are, instead, simply The One.

The reason for the paradox is that we live in an existence which creates the illusion of separation. Deep down, we're all the same One but, for the sake of being able to experience all the drama and excitement that life in this world has to offer, the appearance of separation into the All was created.

This was done so that Infinite Being can observe itself from an infinite variety of viewpoints. That includes your unique viewpoint, my unique viewpoint, and everyone else's unique viewpoints.

Infinite Being created space by creating an infinite number of unique locations within its consciousness, and then projected its consciousness into that space in order to create the universe. In the next chapter, we'll see how this was achieved.

The Dynamics Of Consciousness

The mind of Infinite Being is all there is and all there ever was. The physical universe was created from 100% consciousness and nothing else, because consciousness is the only tool available to Infinite Being.

Remember that Infinite Being originally created three aspects of itself: Thought, Feeling and Motion. By projecting Thought as one type of consciousness and Feeling as a complementary, but different, type of consciousness, it was possible to create different motions and potentials through the interaction of Original Thought and Feeling.

The interaction of Thought and Feeling is intertwined, just like in the electromagnetism that forms light waves. The two types of energy waves operate in different planes of expression and interact with each other at right angles.

Electromagnetic Waves

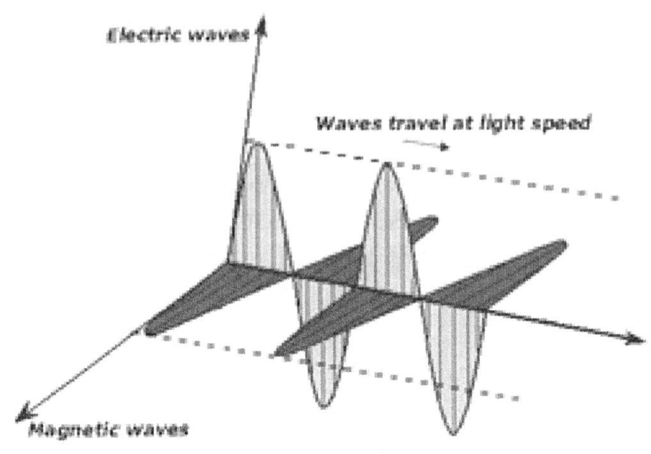

Consciousness works in exactly the same manner. Thought and Feeling are intertwined and set into motion.

Mind Waves

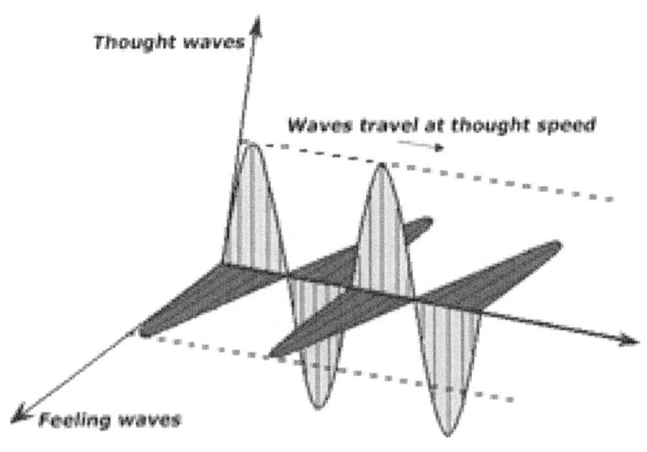

From this creation of dynamic consciousness, different frequencies of consciousness become possible, as do different degrees of compression. The twelve density layers of consciousness in the universe differ in the degrees of compression which have been applied to them. The higher layers are more subtle and more expanded than the tightly-focused, lower layers.

In our third-density, physical existence, we can apply the same formula of creation to develop our own potential into everything that it can become. The formula Thought plus Feeling plus Motion, in the human realm, translates into thought being used to analyze and plan; feeling being employed to bring life into what needs to become manifest; and, finally, action bringing that plan into manifestation.

The existence of this formula of creation shows the potential of human creativity quite clearly. It means, quite simply, that,

You can manifest anything you can imagine.

Celebrate Who You Are

Earlier, we saw how infinite diversity is part of the plan behind the very existence of the universe. Now, we can see how part of the plan of Creation is that each and every one of us will discover and develop the full potential that exists within each of our unique personalities.

Your primary purpose in life is to experience life from one individual, unique point of view. You are an expression of Infinite Being as it experiences itself from all possible viewpoints. The best way you can serve yourself and Infinite Being, the source within us all, is to live your life to your own, personal, highest potential.

Knowing this, we can see that it is no longer acceptable to live under the Old Reality pressure to suppress individual achievement. From an early age, people are typically taught to be overly modest about their own abilities.

People should be encouraged to thrive, grow and prosper in all ways.

Adopting a veneer of modesty in order to avoid sparking jealousy in others is just not acceptable in the New Reality. We contain the ultimate potential within each and every one of us. Different people are programmed by their choice of environment in life to explore different facets of their all-potential.

The New Reality is based upon heart-centered consciousness and, therefore, requires that people support and encourage each other. With heart-centered consciousness, your motive in improving your skills will always be tempered by your desire to serve humanity in the best way possible.

In the Old Reality, it was usual for people to take jobs simply for a selfish reason: They needed the money. In the New Reality, people are finding work in which they can do what they love so that they can love what they do.

If a heart-centered person doesn't have their heart in their job, they get bored very quickly and start looking for work which is meaningful to them. Their new job doesn't have to be something exotic. A person can be very happy working in industries that may sound routine, but in which they find meaningful, rewarding activity making sure that people can get the specific goods and services that they need.

When you meet someone who really loves what they do, their attitude of helpfulness can uplift your day and make everything so much the brighter for the experience. It can touch you so profoundly that it is difficult to forget the experience. Unlike the other extreme of meeting someone who couldn't care less, which can leave you wishing that you *could* forget the experience!

In the New Reality, you have the freedom to celebrate who you are, because you understand that, by design, there is no one exactly like you in the entire universe. The world needs you and the service that you offer, as you help people in your own, unique way.

Remember Your Spiritual Home

The Universal Yearning for Unity is a silent, yet ever-present call towards our spiritual home. As we master the experiences of third-density living and move on to higher density layers, we become more expanded in our awareness and more aware of the enormous scale of Creation.

When you allow your awareness to expand further and further, you can make an imaginary visit to the All That Is, to your original spiritual home.

The planet on which we stand is enormous compared to the size of a human being. Imagine yourself viewing the Earth from a distance. Imagine the silence and peace that permeates your very soul as you look upon the Mother Earth, who has provided all of us with this wonderful home in space.

Then, in your mind's eye, see the Sun. Imagine this brilliant orb and feel its life-giving energy while your mind adjusts to the fact that the Sun is over a million times bigger than the Earth.

Now, expand your viewpoint far enough to see and appreciate your entire solar system. Next, you realize that there are many more suns in our galaxy. In our Milky Way galaxy, there are 200 billion other suns. Expand your viewpoint even more as you imagine yourself seeing an entire galaxy, slowly rotating like a giant disk in the great peace and quietness of space.

Then, you realize that there are many more galaxies in existence. There are well over 100 billion other galaxies in this universe. Now, expand your viewpoint to include the entire universe, filled with billions of galaxies. You realize that, as big as the universe is, in order for God to be everywhere, God has to be even bigger still.

All of this, this All Things, is contained within the consciousness of Infinite Being. Beyond the limits of the universe, beyond the envelope of space, lies only that which created it. The universe is contained within the creative awareness and loving energy of Infinite Being.

As you feel Infinite Being holding the universe within manifestation, and preserving all of life within its infinite field of profound love, you sense what your ultimate potential really is. You sense that all of the universe will one day come back to embrace this, its original spiritual home. This all-knowing, all-feeling, all-present spirit, which is behind all of life as we know it.

Now, as your attention returns to your own space on Planet Earth, you remember that feeling, that sense of wonder, of wisdom, and that awareness of ultimate potential.

And, as you think of your own life, you now understand what it means to be connected to that ultimate inner reality, as...

Infinite Being, infinite potential.

Understanding The Yearning

We all have a Universal Yearning for Unity consciousness, a mission deep inside each of us to return to that from which we came. And, today, that mission has become a top priority.

These are the days of The Shift. The New Reality of spiritually empowered, heart-centered consciousness is emerging. The world is transforming into heart-centered consciousness and it is this very Shift that creates a historical opportunity for spiritual progress.

Now that you understand that the universe was formed from Original Intent and Original Feeling set into motion, you can appreciate that the entire universe is filled with the love of the Creator. We were created in the image, or creative imagination, of the Creator and we feel that love which inspires us to work our way through experience back to that from which we came.

It is love that fills space. It is love that manifests the magnetic fabric of space. Love is the consciousness that holds the universe in manifestation.

The next time you have a feeling that love is in the air, you'll be right. Love *is* in the air. It always was. It is the fabric of space and everything that exists.

It is, literally, love that holds the universe together.

Transformation Into The New Reality

In my first book, *The Shift: The Revolution in Human Consciousness*, I pointed out that the apparent chaos of these changing times is actually good news because it means that you're going through a transformation to a new energy level.

If you resonate a container of water with sound waves that generate a balanced, symmetrical pattern on the surface of the water and then turn up the frequency a little, chaos will ensue. The neat pattern on the surface of the water will become choppy and discordant. However, when you turn the frequency up still more, a new pattern emerges, one which is even more complex and beautiful than the original. Through the temporary transition of chaos, a new, higher frequency has emerged in perfect order and harmony.

No matter what pressures unfold as the frequency of the planet increases, remember that, afterwards, those pressures will start decreasing as the new reality takes hold.

We will soon witness the birth of a loving and beautiful world, and there is not a force in the universe that can stop it.

The unfolding New Reality consciousness opens the door to new vistas of awareness and new levels of creativity. In the dawning New Reality, people follow their hearts to express their inner joy through making their own meaningful and unique contributions towards a better world.

The New Reality will, through heart-centered consciousness, bring the dream of peace and harmony into existence. Quality of life will be measured in how much natural beauty has been created in your surroundings, in how safe you feel to travel anywhere on the planet, in how inspired and creative you feel in your efforts to serve humanity in your own unique way.

In the New Reality, learning, freedom and abundance will be the experience of all people throughout the planet.

The New Reality will bring a harmony among humanity, a sense of connection with, and gratitude for, the Mother Earth and for the unconditional love that constantly streams from the Sun and throughout the Creator's universe.

Being alive in the days of The Shift brings its own reward. Today, we are experiencing this historic, global transformation from basic humanity to spiritual humanity.

The Density Layers Of Existence

Earlier, I asked, "Is it a straight run to the ultimate state of God-consciousness, or is there some stairway to heaven in existence, with each step being a stage along the way?"

There are twelve density layers of consciousness in existence. The higher numbers are more subtle, more expansive in their scale than the lower numbers. Each lower density layer is more compressed than the one above it and it is formed within the one above it.

Some people call these realms *dimensions,* which can cause confusion, as a dimension is actually something else. When referring to the twelve density layers, or realms, the technically accurate term is *density*. A dimension is not a location or a higher realm. A dimension is a measurable component of reality, such as length, width, height or time.

A density is a layer of compressed consciousness. It is a location within Creation. Instead of saying that you live in third density (the physical realm), you can abbreviate it to '3D,' provided you remember that, in this case, '3D' is short for third density, and not for three-dimensional.

The ultimate state of Infinite Being lies beyond twelfth density, as all densities are creations within its consciousness. The twelve density layers exist within the consciousness of Infinite Being.

The densities of immediate application to humanity are third, fourth and fifth densities.

3D: The physical realm

The physical world exists in 3D, or third density. Our minds are not limited to 3D, by any means. The global consciousness will go through a quantum shift when a critical mass in higher consciousness is reached. This critical mass will be achieved by a numerically small portion of the world's population because people with higher frequencies of consciousness have, proportionately, a much greater influence on the global mind atmosphere than do people who operate at lower frequencies of consciousness. As always, it will be the pioneers who change history.

4D: The spirit or astral realm

Throughout recorded history, fourth density has been the spirit or astral realm. 4D can be subdivided into twelve sub-layers or overtones, referred to in the plural as spirit or astral realms. When a person passes on from their physical incarnation, they typically move into residence in the third or fourth overtone of 4D. While physical experience can generate issues of emotional separation, 4D is an integrative density where people work through a healing of their issues. Spiritual seekers soon discover that there are higher, more subtle overtones within 4D and move there to study the higher truths of the universe.

5D: The soul realm

When the time comes to move on from the 4D spirit world, people move up into 5D in order to begin planning the experiences that they want to explore in their next incarnation.

Think of this as a kind of destiny workshop, where all possibilities are examined until, finally, one course of action is decided upon.

In 5D, the viewpoint of the soul is much wider than the focused viewpoint of the conscious mind in 3D. In 5D, space and time are seen as an interwoven tapestry of possibilities. Souls, during their research, can actually insert themselves into any situation in which they are interested, regardless of when and where.

In 5D, you can experience any event at any location and any point in time. You can go back into history or go forward into probable futures. You can view all possible outcomes of every potential situation and how it interacts with the probable actions of others. It works because your soul senses the total energy of each situation, seeing everything that would unfold if it were acted out.

So, in 5D consciousness, you can view exactly how a future event is likely to materialize. You can see it, feel it, touch it and know what your thoughts and feelings will be at that time because you actually insert your consciousness into the experience of the future event.

That leads us, next, to the subject of dynamic life planning and the déjà vu phenomenon.

Dynamic Life Planning

The future is a fickle thing. The plan that you made at a soul level is constantly adjusted and updated as the future unfolds into the present. Normally, your life plan's objectives remain the same as the day you were born, but the details are constantly modified to suit the circumstances of life as they unfold.

Déjà vu occurs when you find yourself experiencing a situation in the 3D physical world that you have seen before in a 5D preview of that situation. At a deeper, soul level of consciousness is the memory of your having seen that exact scene.

You may have previewed that exact situation as long ago as prior to your birth but, more often, it will be one that you reviewed in recent weeks. You review your life plan – your self-made destiny – as often as is necessary to manage the fine details along the way.

Once, in the 1970s, I was about to change jobs and I was very curious as to how it would turn out. I knew what kind of work environment I didn't want any more, and I had many possibilities open to me. My dreamtime at night must have been filled with research into the possibilities, because, as soon as I settled on one particular new job and started work there, déjà vu struck!

The new job was located in a pie-shaped building – one that was built right at the convergence of two streets that merged like a "Y" into one street. The shape of the building meant that some of its rooms were very unusual in shape. One such irregularly shaped room was set up to store technical manuals on wooden shelves.

As I walked into the room for the first time, I recognized the scene. I vividly remembered having seen the stacks of manuals, the unusual wooden shelves and the odd shape of the room somewhere before, just recently. As I stared around in amazement, slowly recovering from the surprise, I began to realize just how much work we must do in our sleep to fine-tune events that are about to occur in the very near future.

Your personal life plan will never be derailed as long as you, at a soul level of consciousness, keep reviewing that plan and adjusting to new options and opportunities as they arise. Even if one door shuts in the corridor of life, there are many more that can open to keep your life on-plan and on-track. Early in every night's sleep, when deep sleep comes the easiest, you have the opportunity to detach from the 3D physical world and pass up through the 4D spirit world on your way to the 5D world of your inner self, your soul consciousness.

Even if the main focus of your attention were to never go and visit 5D while your physical brain sleeps, that part of you will still keep planning, adjusting and working to keep your intention for this life on-track. Just as the subconscious mind manages your bodily functions without any conscious attention from you, so does your superconscious soul perform its function, whether or not you bring the main focus of your attention into mesh with its work at night.

A part of your consciousness is constantly aware of your life plan and is constantly reviewing its progress.

Discovery Through Meditation

The details of your life plan can be discovered through three methods – meditation, dream recall, and intuitive attention.

Meditation has become a very popular answer to the need for balance in today's fast-moving society. Through meditation you contact the most real part of you. This part is the spiritual source which existed before your physical body was formed. Through contact with that reality, the essence of your soul, you become more identified with that inner you. Your inner self is who you really are. Then, you begin to realize more of your potential because you are able to identify what that potential is.

Anyone who has experienced the silent peace of a good, deep meditation knows that consciousness can run a lot deeper than it does during the noise and clatter of everyday experience. Think of the best, most relaxing, most profound meditation you've ever had and you know what it is like to open your heart and then bathe in the peace and wisdom of your inner being.

Your inner being or soul is the fountain of wisdom within you. It has access to all information in the universe because it is consciously connected to the entire universe. Your inner being is your personal connection to Infinite Being. Even when your outer self is busy concentrating on the distractions of the outside world, your inner self is still active, and still connected in all ways.

Through contacting your inner self, you become more aware of your greatest inner joy. When you follow that innermost joy, you consciously resonate with your soul and manifest your true potential in life. This inner resonance enhances your intuition, making you more capable of choosing the best options in life. This increases the synchronicity in your life as you have then achieved a natural flow which is more in harmony with the universe around you.

Most people already have their own favorite meditation style or method. The important components of a meditation which will produce specific intuitive information are as follows:

1. Intent. Set your intention with a mental statement, such as, "I am becoming more and more aware of my complete life plan." Keep the statement in the present, not the future ("I am," not, "I will.")

2. Relax. Close out the outside world by turning off distractions and closing your eyes. Sit upright in a chair and go silently within. Use deep, controlled breathing – equal in breaths and out breaths through the nose – to relax, while focusing your mind by mentally repeating your affirmation phrase with each inbreath.

3. Listen. When you are relaxed, you are in a state of enhanced awareness. The focus of your mind has expanded to include a wider range of inner consciousness. Alert attention is the key. When an intuitive thought comes, it will be a quick flash of understanding; one which unravels within your mind into a complete package of information. You can probe into the package to see if you have perceived all of it. You can ask questions to your inner being for clarification and more information.

The Dream Recall Method

The deepest levels of sleep typically occur in the first two or three hours of sleep. During deep sleep your spirit body can travel to higher states of consciousness and become immersed in routine, life planning adjustments at a soul level of consciousness.

The lighter states of sleep occur later in the sleep cycle. Here, you are much closer to the physical realm and it is here that emotional issues are often worked through and resolved. The key to understanding dreams is that they are composed of symbols, rather than actual people, places and objects. When you focus on the emotion that the dream evoked, then you can unravel how the symbols in the dream played out the emotional tension that you were working through.

Basically, the light dreaming state is an echo chamber of the last three or four days-worth of emotional pressures, worked through as symbols in dreams. The dream sequence can be for balance and healing, or it can be for exploring alternate future possibilities so that you can choose which one you prefer.

You can develop dream recall by keeping a dream diary beside your bed. When you awaken each morning, or at any time of the night, time is of the essence. Each second that you are consciously awake, those dream memories are fast receding, out of reach, into the background. So, before you do anything else at all, write your dreams down in as much detail as you can.

With practice, you will bring the lessons of your dreams closer into your daily waking awareness and recall the deeper dreams as well as the lighter ones. In the deeper dreaming state, you are traveling the 4D spirit realms to communicate with friends, to explore anything that interests your curiosity, and to travel beyond, into the 5D soul realm.

You can gain great insights into the events of your physical life when you tell yourself, each night before bed, that you will remember what you learned while you were out of your body and cruising the other realms of consciousness. You can also go to sleep asking yourself a specific question, like, "What is the most important part of my life plan right now?" That way, you pre-program the action of your nocturnal explorations to something specific. Just be prepared for the answers to be symbolic, not literal, and ready for translation into what these symbols mean to you in your physical awareness.

Symbols are the language of the soul.

How to Tune Into Your Inner Knowing

It's a rare person who can instantly translate the 5D thoughts of their soul into 3D physical words because the translation has to go through, not one, but two density layers. So, defining your exact purpose in life, in a concise summary, can be more of an art than a science.

However, here is a shortcut that delivers fast results.

To translate the 5D awareness of your soul into action in the 3D physical world, use your heart as a 4D interface. Your heart resonates to the frequency band of fourth density.

Lift your awareness into your heart chakra, feel the love, leave the stresses of the day behind, and just tune in.

Tune in to the knowingness of your inner self. As your personal plan evolves each day to suit the new conditions of each day, take the time to tune in within. It just takes a minute, literally, to detach from the outer world and sense the flow that is optimum for you right at that very moment.

The more in tune you become with your inner self, the more you will discover and become familiar with your overall purpose and your plan for that purpose.

Tune into your inner knowing and live your purpose.

Why Following Your Inner Joy Works

The well-used phrase, "Follow your inner joy," is actually a vital key to following your purpose. Once you tune into and follow your inner excitement, then synchronicity starts to flow. Synchronicity is the universe's way of telling you that you're on the right track for your destiny to unfold.

Synchronicity is a flow of events where everything clicks into place to support your efforts. It brings you opportunities, people, events and circumstances exactly when and where they need to be. This all happens because your efforts are harmonious. The universe is naturally harmonious. It has to be that way, in order to function successfully. Harmony is balance, while disharmony is a dysfunction that makes a system fall apart. The universe will naturally support your efforts when they are in harmony, or "in the flow."

Your powerful, day-to-day working tool is to tune into your inner knowing and live your purpose.

Ask yourself, "What is the most exciting thing that I could possibly be doing right now to enhance my innermost joy?"

Within you lies your deepest, inner joy. This innermost joy is something long-term and deeply significant to you. Needless to say, discernment saves lost effort here. Your innermost joy is not something short-term or superficial that might feel good temporarily. Obviously, cravings and comforts don't count.

Then, find a way to do that most exciting possibility. And when you have finished doing that, ask yourself the same question again. Usually, the answer will be something in the same direction as your first act, although not always.

Inner joy is your barometer of natural flow. Use it to determine what action is the most important in developing your experience of life. Find ways to dissolve self-limiting barriers so that you can act upon that inner joy.

To follow your inner joy is to live holistically because you are acting with more of your complete self. It lightens up your spirit, allowing you to function at a higher frequency of consciousness.

By developing a habit of intuitive attention, you keep your conscious mind open to more intuitive feedback. When you wake up each and every morning, remember that you hold the master key to the reason for life itself. Feel the sense of purpose and destiny that will be yours each and every day. Tune into the flow that is ideal for you that day and go into action. Inspired action.

To manifest your full potential:

Tune into your inner knowing, follow your highest joy, and live your purpose.

The Creation Principle

As we covered earlier, *Thought plus feeling in motion* is the underlying formula in the Creation of the universe. When expanded, this principle can also help us uncover and develop our purpose in life.

In the field of human endeavor, the Law of Creation can be expressed in a more human-centric form. The formula for the Creation Principle as applied to human experience can be defined as:

Creation = Intention + Attraction + Motion

While these three elements form the basis of the Creation Principle, it is often further extended in its reach by combining the elements together.

This combination of the three Creation Principle elements of Intention, Attraction, and Motion produces nine combinations, expressed as follows.

1. Intention-Intention, or Intention focused through a lens of Intention
2. Intention-Attraction, or Intention focused through a lens of Attraction.
3. Intention-Motion, or Intention focused through a lens of Motion.
4. Attraction-Intention, or Attraction focused through a lens of Intention.

5. Attraction-Attraction, or Attraction focused through a lens of Attraction.
6. Attraction-Motion, or Attraction focused through a lens of Motion.
7. Motion-Intention, or Motion focused through a lens of Intention.
8. Motion-Attraction, or Motion focused through a lens of Attraction.
9. Motion-Motion, or Motion focused through a lens of Motion.

Next, we will see how this expanded Creation Principle produces *the 9-Step On-Purpose method.*

The 9-Step On-Purpose Method

This in-depth method makes it possible for your true purpose in life to be perfectly expressed and achieved.

The nine combinations of the Creation Principle express in the 9-Step On-Purpose Method as follows:

1. Create (Intention focused through a lens of Intention)

You can create a desired object or reality in your imagination but, for this method, you don't actually do *anything* in Step 1 other than alert your soul that you see purpose guidance. The work of the Intention stage will be done for you at the soul level of your consciousness. Your soul consciousness will create an intention that will help you continue along the path of purpose you have chosen for this life. Step 2 will reveal the Intention.

2. Attune (Intention focused through a lens of Attraction)

Tune into guidance from your soul or higher consciousness by thinking about what course of action would most align with your highest joy at this moment. To give yourself the best support in this vital step, first put yourself in a calm, receptive meditation mode. This is a time for reflective pondering as to what truly constitutes your highest joy and, therefore, *most resonates with the signal* that your soul consciousness is providing to your physical mind.

3. Act (Intention focused through a lens of Motion)

Take action. Take this task as far as you can to the best of your ability. Action places the mental and emotional energy into the physical realm, which is where results happen. We are the physical agents of our souls. Without our physical action, all things remain as unfulfilled potential. *Wishing* a result will not make it so. Physical action will. Action is living out your excitement. In fact, the task doesn't even feel like work because it's what you most want to be doing right now.

4. Build (Attraction focused through a lens of Intention)

Notice how the action you are taking builds a greater sense of purpose in your path through life.

5. Adapt (Attraction focused through a lens of Attraction)

Notice synchronistic changes that are drawn into your life. These "coincidences" reveal what you need to do to adapt, when to adapt, and with whom.

6. Harmonize (Attraction focused through a lens of Motion)

In this step, FLOW is created. The path traveled then becomes the easiest path - the one of greatest harmony and least resistance.

7. Gain Insight (Motion focused through a lens of Intention)

Deeper insight into your path of action is gained in this step. Choose to define any situations that now arise in a positive framework in order to generate a positive effect. In time, this positive viewpoint will be seen to serve your needs to greatest benefit even when events may seem to be at their most challenging. As the Renaissance friar Giovanni Giocondo wrote in 1513, "Everything we call a trial, a sorrow, or a duty, believe me... the gift is there and the wonder of an overshadowing presence."

8. Grow (Motion focused through a lens of Attraction)

Growth can simply be the phase of a project or it can be the result of releasing blockages that interfere with your highest joy. You can redefine your mental definitions as choices in order to release blockages. You can make a negative belief reveal itself by asking the question, "Why should I NOT pursue this path?" Don't base what your idea of what you can be on your past viewpoints.

Release old definitions and allow new growth to occur.

9. Complete (Motion focused through a lens of Motion)

As blockages are dissolved, the momentum of your intended path becomes optimal and your true purpose is perfectly achieved.

Follow up

Make a note of the steps in the 9-Step On-Purpose Method and use that as your point of reference to observe your progress:

1. Create
2. Attune
3. Act
4. Build
5. Adapt
6. Harmonize
7. Gain Insight
8. Grow
9. Complete

About The Author

Owen Waters is the author of several books, including *The Shift: The Revolution in Human Consciousness*, available at Amazon.com. As an internationally acclaimed spiritual teacher, Owen Waters has presented his insights into the New Reality to hundreds of thousands of seekers. For more than fifty years, his life has been focused upon a continual search for spiritual answers through research, and through the development of his inner vision.

Today, as Editor and cofounder of InfiniteBeing.com, he writes a free newsletter which promotes a philosophy of spiritual empowerment through inner connection to the source of ultimate human potential.

Also, at InfiniteBeing.com, you can discover a selection of articles and e-books on spiritual metaphysics for the New Reality:

https://www.InfiniteBeing.com

Made in United States
North Haven, CT
23 November 2022